WAR PLANES

Attack Helicopters:
The AH-64 Apaches

by Bill Sweetman

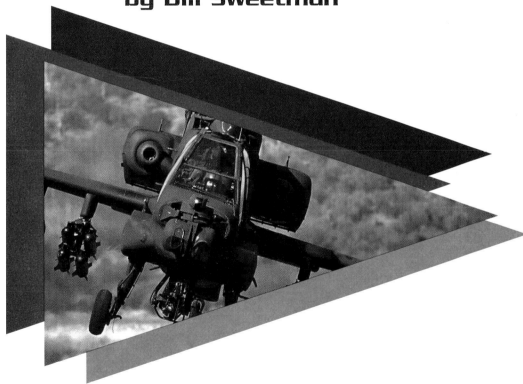

CAPSTONE
HIGH-INTEREST
BOOKS

an imprint of Capstone Press
Mankato, Minnesota

Capstone High-Interest Books are published by Capstone Press
151 Good Counsel Drive, P.O. Box 669, Mankato, Minnesota 56002
http://www.capstone-press.com

Library of Congress Cataloging-in-Publication Data
Sweetman, Bill.
    Attack helicopters: the AH-64 Apaches/by Bill Sweetman.
    p. cm.—(War Planes)
    Includes bibliographical references and index.
    ISBN 0-7368-0789-6
    1. Apache (Attack helicopter)—Juvenile literature. [1. Apache (Attack
helicopter) 2. Helicopters.] I. Title. II. War Planes (Mankato, Minn.)
UG1232.A88 S93 2001
623.7'464—dc21   00-010399

Summary: Discusses the AH-64 Apache helicopter, its uses, engines, weapons,
and future in the U.S. Army.

Editorial Credits
Matt Doeden, editor; Lois Wallentine, product planning editor; Timothy
    Halldin, cover designer and illustrator; Katy Kudela, photo researcher

Photo Credits
Boeing Management Company, cover, 1, 4, 6, 9, 10, 12, 23, 24, 28
Photri-Microstock, 18
Ted Carlson/Fotodynamics, 16–17, 20, 26

Consultant
Major Scott D. Ross, Public Affairs Office, U.S. Army Aviation Center

1 2 3 4 5 6 06 05 04 03 02 01

Table of Contents

Chapter One

Learn About

- The Apache's mission
- Apache history
- Apache models

The Apache in Action

It is late at night over the desert. A group of
U.S. soldiers is moving toward an enemy camp.
But the soldiers are in danger. Ahead, an enemy
tank moves slowly and quietly toward them.

Miles away, eight dark green helicopters
fly above the desert toward the U.S. soldiers.
The helicopters are Boeing AH-64 Apaches.
They belong to the U.S. Army. The Apaches'
special sensors allow their pilots to see
well in the dark.

The Apache is an attack helicopter.

The enemy tank moves closer to the soldiers. It will soon be in range to fire at them. But the soldiers hear the roar of the Apache helicopters before the tank can attack. The Apaches fly over the soldiers toward the enemy tank. Gunners aboard the helicopters target the enemy tank and fire their missiles.

For a moment, the flames from the missiles' exhaust light the sky. The missiles then strike and destroy the enemy tank. The U.S. soldiers are safe.

Building the Apache

During the Vietnam War (1954–1975), the U.S. military used jet fighters to attack enemy ground troops. But much of Vietnam was covered by a thick jungle. Jet pilots flew over the jungle at speeds of about 600 miles (970 kilometers) per hour. They could not see their targets.

The U.S. military needed a better attack aircraft. Army pilots fitted troop-carrying helicopters with rockets and machine guns. The helicopters worked better as attack aircraft than the jets had. The helicopters could fly lower and at slower speeds. But military officials wanted an attack helicopter built just for attack missions. The officials wanted an attack helicopter that could carry guided missiles. It also wanted a helicopter that could safely fly close to the ground.

The U.S. military began planning such a helicopter in 1973. Military officials hired a company called McDonnell Douglas to design and build the helicopters. This company is now part of the Boeing company. Officials named the helicopter the AH-64 Apache. The Apaches took a long time to build. The U.S. Army received its first Apaches in 1984.

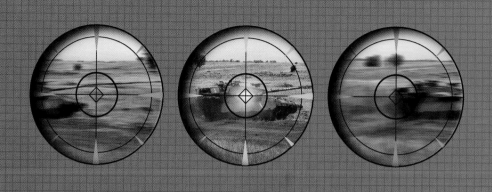

About the Apache

The Boeing AH-64 Apache is the world's most heavily armed attack helicopter. Today, more than 1,000 Apaches are in service around the world. The United States is not the only country to use them. Countries such as Great Britain, the Netherlands, and Israel also use Apaches.

The U.S. Army has two kinds of Apaches. The AH-64A is the main model. But the military also has a special model of the Apache. This model is the AH-64D Longbow. The Longbow is an improved version of the AH-64A model. Its weapons and sensors are more advanced than those on the AH-64A.

More than 1,000 Apaches are used around the world.

Learn About

→ The Apache's design
→ The Apache's controls
→ Apache armor

Inside the Apache

The Apache does not look like most helicopters. It has a narrow body. The sides are blocklike. Short wings are attached to its sides. The wings carry racks of rockets and missiles.

The Apache has a unique look because of how it fights and flies. In combat, the Apache flies fewer than 100 feet (30 meters) above the ground. Its narrow body makes the Apache a small target for enemy fire. The Apache rarely has to fly fast. Its blocklike sides carry armor. This makes the Apache tough and durable.

The main rotor is above and behind the cockpit.

Engines and Rotors

The Apache is powered by two General Electric T700 turboshaft engines. A turboshaft engine creates hot air to turn the helicopter's rotors. Each of the Apache's engines produces almost 1,700 horsepower. This is more power than the engines of four Corvette cars can produce.

The Apache's turboshaft engines have special jetpipes. The jetpipes mix the hot gas from the engines with the cooler air outside. This keeps the engine's temperature down. A cool engine temperature hides the Apache from infrared sensors. These sensors detect objects by their heat.

The Apache has two rotors. The main rotor is behind and above the cockpit. This rotor includes four rotor blades. The blades allow the pilot to lift and steer the helicopter. The tail rotor sits on the Apache's tail. Pilots use the tail rotor to turn.

Inside the Cockpit

Each Apache carries two crewmembers. The crewmembers sit in the cockpit. The pilot sits in the back seat. The co-pilot gunner (CPG) sits in front of the pilot. The Apache's narrow body gives both crewmembers a good view to both sides.

The pilot controls the main rotor with two control sticks. One stick changes the pitch of all of the rotor blades. The pitch is the angle of the blades. Changing the pitch of the blades makes the Apache move up and down. The second stick changes the pitch of the rotor disk. This change in angle moves the helicopter forward and backward.

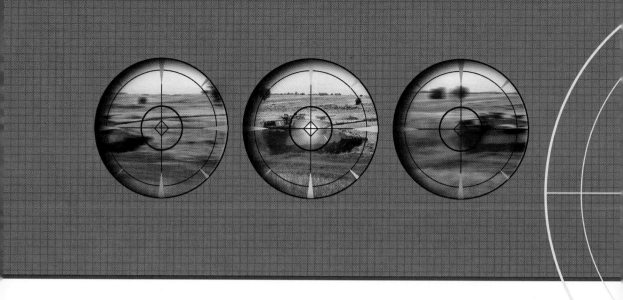

The pilot uses pedals to control the tail rotor. The pedals control a turn's rate and direction.

Safety Features

The Apache is difficult to shoot down. The helicopter's most important mechanical parts are strong enough to keep working after they are hit. For example, the main rotor gearbox can lose all of its oil and keep running. It runs long enough to allow the pilot to land safely.

The Apache can fly with only one engine. The engines are on opposite sides of the helicopter's body. One hit will rarely destroy both of them. The Apache's fuel tanks are sealed with a special liner. The liner seals any holes in the tanks caused by enemy weapons.

The Apache's crew also is protected. Sheets of lightweight armor protect the crew seats. This

Apache Specifications

Function:	Multi-Mission Combat Helicopter
Manufacturer:	Boeing McDonnell Douglas Helicopter Systems
Date Deployed:	1984
Length:	58 feet (17.7 meters)
Wing Span:	17 feet, 2 inches (5.2 meters)
Height:	15 feet, 3 inches (4.6 meters)
Weight:	11,800 pounds (5,352 kilograms)
Payload:	3,275 pounds (1,485 kilograms)
Engine:	Two T700-GE-701Cs
Speed:	232 miles (374 kilometers) per hour
Range:	1,180 miles (1,900 kilometers) with external fuel

armor protects crewmembers from most bullets. The Apache also is designed to protect crewmembers in case of a crash. The helicopter's landing gear and lower body give way during a crash. This softens the impact for the crewmembers. Crewmembers can survive a crash straight down at speeds as fast as 30 miles (48 kilometers) per hour.

main rotor hub

cockpit

rocket pod

M230 gun

Hellfire missile

The AH-64 Apache

main rotor blade

tail rotor

engine

tail wheel

Chapter Three

Learn About

- Gunner control
- The AGM-114 Hellfire missile
- Hydra rockets

Weapons and Tactics

The Apache is designed to be an attack aircraft. Its weapons are its most important features. Apache pilots and CPGs work together to destroy enemy targets and to protect ground troops. Each Apache can carry missiles, rockets, and a machine gun to help crews complete missions.

The Hellfire missile is the Apache's most deadly weapon.

Quick Strike

In combat, the Apache pops up quickly from
behind trees and hills. Crewmembers fire its
weapons and then drop back out of sight.

Apache pilots and CPGs have equipment that allows them to locate targets and fire quickly. Crewmembers wear a special kind of helmet during missions. The helmet is connected to the helicopter's computer system. Sensors inside the helmet tell the computer when and where the crewmember's head turns. The computer can lock onto any target that the pilot or CPG looks at. Crewmembers do not have to spend much time aiming their weapons. They can just look and fire.

Guns

The Apache has a machine gun turret under its nose. This turret is linked to infrared sensors and special cameras that help the CPG find targets. The turret moves automatically with the movement of the CPG's head. The CPG needs only to look at the target and fire the guns.

The Apache carries an M230 machine gun. This gun is mounted under the helicopter. The M230 shoots up to 625 bullets per minute.

Missiles and Rockets

The Apache's most important weapon is the AGM-114 Hellfire missile. The Hellfire is a laser-guided missile. The Apache's CPG points a laser beam at a target. The crew then fires the Hellfire missile. The missile includes sensors that detect the laser beam. The Hellfire then strikes the beam's target.

The Hellfire is the Apache's tank-killing weapon. It is an air-to-ground missile. The Hellfire includes a 17-pound (7.7-kilogram) warhead. This explosive is powerful enough to destroy even the toughest tank armor. Apaches can carry as many as 16 Hellfire missiles. But some carry only eight.

Apaches also carry 2.75-inch (7-centimeter) Hydra rockets. These powerful explosives fly like missiles. But Hydra rockets are not guided. They fly in a straight line. They carry many small explosives called bomblets.

Apache crewmembers fire rockets at enemies.

Chapter Four

Learn About

- Longbow improvements
- Computer datalinks
- Future usefulness

The Future

The Apache has been the Army's most important attack helicopter since it came into service in 1984. The U.S. military has used it in almost every major conflict since then. It still is the most heavily armed and effective attack helicopter in service today.

The U.S. military is working to improve its Apaches. It is adding modern computers and sensors in some Apaches. It also is buying more AH-64D Longbows.

All of the Army's new Apaches are Longbows.

The Longbow

All of the U.S. military's new Apaches are AH-64D Longbows. These helicopters have an improved radar system. The new radar system helps pilots to better track multiple targets.

Crews also can locate targets while flying through heavy smoke. The radar system is connected to the helicopter's computers. The computers determine information such as the location and size of each target. Computers display this information on monitors for Apache crewmembers.

The Longbow Apache also has a sensitive radio receiver. It picks up signals from enemy radar devices. Enemies may use radar to locate and shoot down Apaches. The Apache's computers show enemy radar on the monitor.

Updated Systems

The Longbow carries several new and updated weapons. One of these weapons is a new type of Hellfire missile. The new missile is not guided by a laser. Instead, it has a small radar device in

Experts say the Apache will be useful until at least 2020.

its nose. The radar guides the missile to its target. This feature allows Apache CPGs to fire more than one missile at a time. The CPGs do not have to wait for a missile to strike its target before moving a laser beam.

Apaches often perform missions in groups. Longbows use a datalink to communicate. This radio connection allows all of the helicopters in a group to instantly share computer information. For example, one Longbow may rise up to attack. Its computer sends all the information it gathers to the other Longbows in the team. This allows crewmembers in the other helicopters to select targets even before they can see them.

The U.S. Army plans to make more improvements to the Apache in the future. The helicopters may get more powerful engines. This would increase the Apache's top speed. They also could get a quieter rotor system. This system would allow pilots to better sneak up on enemies. Military experts believe that the Apache will remain the U.S. military's best attack helicopter until at least 2020.

Words to Know

armor (AR-mur)—a protective metal covering

datalink (DAY-tuh-lingk)—a radio connection that allows computers aboard aircraft to share information

laser beam (LAY-zur BEEM)—a narrow, intense beam of light

mission (MISH-uhn)—a military task

pitch (PICH)—the angle of the blades on a helicopter rotor; pitch determines whether a helicopter moves up or down.

radar (RAY-dar)—equipment that uses radio waves to locate and guide objects

rotor (ROH-tur)—machinery that spins a set of rotating blades; rotors allow helicopter pilots to lift or steer an aircraft.

turboshaft (TUR-boh-shaft)—a kind of engine that produces hot air to turn helicopter rotors

turret (TUR-it)—a mount on a helicopter that holds a gun; turrets turn so that guns can be fired in different directions.

warhead (WOR-hed)—the explosive part of a missile

To Learn More

Green, Michael. *The United States Army.* Serving Your Country. Mankato, Minn.: Capstone High-Interest Books, 1998.

Pitt, Matthew. *Apache Helicopter: The AH-64.* High-Tech Military Weapons. New York: Children's Press, 2000.

Schleifer, Jay. *Combat Helicopters.* Wings. Mankato, Minn.: Capstone Books, 1996.

Useful Addresses

San Diego Aerospace Museum
2001 Pan American Plaza
Balboa Park
San Diego, CA 92101

U.S. Army Public Affairs
1500 Army Pentagon
Washington, DC 20310-1500

Internet Sites

Army Technology—AH-64A/D Apache
http://www.army-technology.com/projects/apache

Military Analysis Network—AH-64 Apache
http://www.fas.org/man/dod-101/sys/ac/ah-64.htm

U.S. Army
http://www.army.mil

Index